Singing in the Key of L

Poems by

Barbra Nightingale

1999 Winner, NFSPS Stevens Poetry Manuscript Award

NFSPS Press
Rochester Hills, MI

This publication is the 1999 winner of the National Federation of State Poetry Society Stevens Poetry Manuscript Competition. Publication does not constitute endorsement in ideas or language by the NFSPS. Rather, it specifically endorses the idea of freedom of speech on the part of the poet, and of the autonomy of the judge who selected the winning manuscript, principles we believe to be important for all literary competitions. While a poem may not reflect the tastes of some of our membership, we believe strongly that poets must remain uncensored.

This competition is an annual competition with a deadline of October 15th. Complete rules and information on the purchase of past publications may be obtained by contacting Amy Zook, NFSPS Stevens Poetry Manuscript Chairman, 3520 St. Rd 56, Mechanicsburg, Ohio 43044.

Copyright © Barbra Nightingale, 1999

ISBN   0-9671810-0-3

Library of Congress Catalog Card Number 99-62715

Cover Design: Bruce Stawicki
http://members.tripod.com/bstawic2

Published by the National Federation of State Poetry Societies
NFSPS Press
3128 Walton Blvd. PMB 186
Rochester Hills, MI 48309

Acknowledgments

Grateful acknowledgment is made to the following journals where these poems first appeared:

Birmingham Poetry Review: "Playing for Keeps"
California Quarterly: "Pedestals"
California State Quarterly: "Archaeology"
Cathartic:: "Don't Underestimate the Power of Moonlight"
Cogitative Reveries: "Singing in the Key of L"
Liberty Hill Poetry Journal: "Creating Our Past"
Many Mountains Moving: "One Night Stand"
Mediphors: "Interdental Processes"
PN Magazine: "Insomnia 2"
Sunscripts: "Eventually"
The Chatahoochee Review: "Becoming Beautiful, But Going Mad"
The MacGuffin: "Sleeping with the Ants"
Urban Spaghetti: "Abracadabra"

The following poems appeared in *Lunar Equations* (©Barbra Nightingale, 1993, East Coast Editions): "Don't Underestimate the Power of Moonlight," "Insomnia 2," "Lost Phases," "Singing in the Key of L."

I wish to thank my family, especially my mother, Jeri Evans, my brothers, Michael, Steven, and Alex Evans, and my daughter Kim. I owe several friends a debt of gratitude: Magi, Gary, Judy, Larry, Peter, Margo, and Lola for their help, support and encouragement. For everyone at Broward Community College, a thank you for putting up with me all these years, and for the Hannah Kahn Poetry Foundation, the Florida State and National Poetry Foundations, and the South Florida Poetry Institute for their dedication and support in fostering poetry everywhere. A special thank you for Betty Owen, who has always believed in me, and a remembrance for my father, Arthur Evans.

Introduction

I came back to Singing in the Key of L again and again. I picked it out initially—and then as I read and reread, came to define the things that made this manuscript the one I chose to win the competition. First, I like the cohesiveness of the entire manuscript. It forms a whole. It is more than a collection of poems. It comments on the centrality of music in our culture and plays with the historical notion of singing—the idea that there is a "Singer," who in certain societies/cultures has addressed health/healing/dis-ease in, by, and through singing. Many aboriginal tribes had a "Singer" whose job it was to "sing" out illness. We remember that the Old English poem, "Caedmon's Hymn" was, in fact, a song. Singing is an important part of most religious services—and the entire manuscript is organized around and demonstrates the importance of singing. Of course there is the modern model, the poet, Walt Whitman, who says: "I sing myself." What stands out in this manuscript is the author's addition of the letter L and the way that it conjoins music and language.

The first thing a reader/editor sees when picking up a manuscript or poem is the title of the piece. Obviously this author has given thought to the title of this work. It intrigues, invites the reader to think and to want to know more. The title does some work. It plays with language. It privileges certain words and concepts, and it conflates music and language/writing, singing and saying. Since there is no actual key of L in music, the reader is invited to make connections that will be played out and played upon throughout the entire work. Language and linguistics, love and loss, and as the poet says in the title poem: "lousy, limp lame," sounds that sound like 'ell" all attest to the importance of singing "loud, lusty, loud and free," in inventing new chords . . .

I am also attracted to the voice of the poet that comes across as authentic. I would like to address the initial poem in the book here. It follows after the epigraph that alludes to knowing people. The reader is readily captivated by the 'I' or speaker of the initial poem. In the first couple of lines of the poem, the writer gets the reader's attention with a command and response: "You order me to write/And like a good girl I listen." I am aware here that there is some sort of history that actually occurs before the action of the poem has begun. There has been an order to write. I am interested in this you who gives such an order and interested in the "good girl" who listens. The use of the word listens is important since we listen not only to music, but something is happening in the poem because the girl is listening.

Another element that comes to the fore in this poem and in the collection as a whole is the play of language, of linguistics. The author turns the reader's attention to language and to the fact that place is related to and defines language-and music as well. Implied but not stated is what music stands for: "The best way to get to knowing . . . is to go and listen to . . . music."

Ideas that marvelously come together as the poem moves toward its close are the notion of language as talking -and of what occurs when the speaker says: "I've stopped talking to you,/I'm speaking about him." A wonderful shift happens here; the poet juxtaposes "talking to" and "talking about"—both stressing the significance of language. There is, again, a fine representation of synaesthesia: "He says I taste like summer." Then we note what he says; he tells, "with conviction/with his eyes, his hands, his tongue" that the "good girl" is "beautiful." But whoa! Let's think back to the title of the poem: "Becoming Beautiful But Going Mad." And we learn that Madness: "is my only solace, my prize./I wear it like a silk dress."

The ending of the poem is sound and sure. It brings unity to the idea prefigured in the title. "Endings are only beginnings in disguise." We're thrown into language again, into imperfect words where "a vowel then a consonant/ then another and another" always follow and where "No one ever has the last word." Well, "somewhere there's a song about that," the author/"good girl" has noted, and the poem is that song.

Finally, to jump to the final poem in the collection, the poet reminds the reader that: we are always "Creating Our Past, a past that is also our future. As T.S. Eliot says in Four Quartets: "In the end is our beginning."

It is a pleasure to read such a well-crafted symphony of words. The music of what happens—to borrow the title of Helen Vendler's book on poems, poets, and critics that borrows the words of the Irish poet, Seamus Heaney, the components of this work are never haphazard; they resonate in a play of poetic aesthetics of sound and sense, revealing that who one is is part of where one is. The final epigraph by Jacques Barzun brings us full circle to the Guthrie epigraph: "The best way to get to knowing people is to listen to their music." As Barzun states, "Music is ineffable; it can only be . . . inhaled by the spirit"—as the reader is who listens to Singing in the Key of L.

—Sue Walker

1999 Contest Judge
Editor, *Negative Capability*

Contents

I. A cappella

Becoming Beautiful But Going Mad	1
Master Plan	3
Defining the Blues	4
Don't Underestimate the Power of Moonlight	5
Insomnia 2	6
Lost Phases	8
Appassionato	9
Interdental Processes	10
Just Killing Time	11
Twelve Steps	12
I'm a Woman	14
Celestial Conversations	16
Redemption	17
Concentricities	18
Singing in the Key of L	20

II. Duet

Eventually	23
Cybergames	24
Abracadabra	25
One Night Stand	26
A Million Names for Rain	27
Is the Middle Halfway In	28
Changing the Direction of Dawn	30
Making Love to a Cannibal	31
Mid-life Crisis #23	32
The Other Woman	34
Etude (for Love)	35
Tornado Warning	36
Playing for Keeps	37
The Cape Was Never White	38
Sonnet in Eight Beats	39
Looking Back	40
Storm Warnings	41

III. Cantata

Proverb: If You Have Nothing Good To Say	45
Finding Myself in New Smyrna	46
Sleeping with the Ants	47
Just the Rain Saying It All	49
Pedestals	50
Folding In	51
The Woman Who Talked	52
Archaeology	53
Mutating Shapes	54
Obsession Between the Sheets	55
Song of the Graiae	57
The Philosopher Mechanic	60
Creating Our Past	62

Singing in the Key of L

All songs are poems, but not all poems can be sung.

All music is folk music. I ain't never heard a horse sing a song.

—Louis Armstrong

For Joshua

I. *A cappella*

The best way to get to knowing any bunch of people is to go and listen to their music. —Woody Guthrie

Becoming Beautiful But Going Mad

You order me to write
and like a good girl I listen.
The night is cool
and tastes of salt.
I have just finished
your latest book
and want to cry.
I wish I were Latin
or Greek, someone
with a history
wider than my own.
Even the crickets know
a language I can't imagine.
I try talking to my cat,
holding her intensely.
She scratches my arm
and twists out of reach.
She sits like a statue
and stares at me coldly.
I know she thinks I am to blame:
I don't know her language either.

*

So why is it we say the night
is full of stars? Don't we remember
so is the day? You can
see them. Close your eyes.
They speak Portuguese.

*

In a poem you said music
was mathematical. You forgot
to say love. Everything depends
on music and love.
Imagine a world with no music,
no sound. A **equals** B.
That's why when you take it apart
you are left with nothing.
Somewhere there's a song about that.

*

In the same poem you said
"Only the truly beautiful go mad."
That's what you called it.
What do you call a night
as light as day?

*

It is summer. No, winter.
How can we tell? Here in the tropics
the heat drives us mad.
It is carried by mosquitoes.
The madness, not the heat.
Perhaps both.
I have listened to the wind tell stories,
the trees drop their leaves like applause.
When will they start spinning?
What is snow?

*

My skin is the color of raw almonds,
smooth and beige with a yellow tint.
I've stopped talking to you,
I'm speaking about him.
He says I taste like summer.
It is no wonder. It is always summer.
He is the only one who tells me with conviction
with his eyes, his hands, his tongue:
I am beautiful. And mad.
It is my only solace, my prize.
I wear it like a silk dress.
Endings are only beginnings in disguise.
Something always follows.
A vowel then a consonant

then another and another.
No one ever has the last word.

Master Plan
Snow White

She was always jealous of me
even before the mirror spoke,
enraged at what people thought.
Little did she know
my heart was as black as hers.

Everyone felt sorry for me
slaving after those dwarves
but truth is the other way around.
I was waited on hand and foot—
even the Queen had not such care.

I didn't want to leave. Why would I?
If it took seven to make one whole,
well that was better than none,
and when that wimpy prince arrived,
I could see none were better than one.

That was the root of her anger.
That I could choose.
Married to my father,
she was trapped in her own web,
trading herself for power.

Ok, so maybe I did know
who was knocking on my door,
had some need to confront her.
True, I lost every time,
but oh! She had to look!

Knowing how the story would end
I almost felt sorry for her—
dancing herself to death
spinning deeper and deeper
ashes   ashes   everywhere.

Defining the Blues

It is a cold, rainy night,
it is the wind that presses its breath
into the back of your neck,
it is the yellow stain of a street lamp,
the hum of electric current.
It is slate blue or pale gray,
and tastes like your first cigarette
in four days, rank and dark,
filled with risk.
It clings to your skin like silk
on a summer's day
It is blood thrumming
a rhythm you can follow.
It is the tears that fall
from eyes that say
exactly what they see.
It is the heart that needs to love
beating through the night.

Don't Underestimate the Power of Moonlight

Its pale blue light will drive you mad,
wake you up like dawn,
fill your rooms with shadows,
lead you to acquaintances
better left unknown.

Its spell is irresistible,
rivers, lakes, oceans
follow its direction,
moving to silent rhythms
we know nothing about.
Even our blood tides
sunk deep within our cells
answer the call of lunar equations,
gently rolling to shores of skin.

Listen! You can almost hear
the roar of blood
rushing to reclaim its lost land,
see the erosion as bone by bone
it is carried back into itself
building a reef no tide can cross.

Insomnia 2

It grows late.
The ocean stops
rushing to shore, adopts
the half moon's slow drift
to the other horizon.

Someone drifts
into sleep, whatever
is in his hand, escapes:
pen, book, heart
of a loved one.

In the almost morning
no sound breaks through
windows closed against heat
though there must be crickets,
birds, a howl at moonset.

Watch your dreams, they say,
for signs: broken
toys, houses, patterns of air,
what you seek, have always sought
lies in images locked in the dark.

But to dream is to surrender
to darkness, give in and be lost,
wandering forever in moonlight,
forgetting the beauty in being awake,
the truth in the color of night,
silence of thought.

In this quiet, this wakeful
room, knowledge blossoms,
an often deadly nightshade,
the lure of white petals
stronger than fear,
bolder than dreams.

The twang of the stars,
the hum of the planets,
the grinding rotation of earth,

chases sleep into corners,
and those kept listening
lose nothing important.

Lost Phases

There are secrets not even I will tell:
shadows thrown into corners
balled up like a blue shirt
rank with yesterday's sweat
hidden in the dimmed bedroom,
the lightless spaces under the bed.

Toward dawn you can see them move,
hear them moan as if lost in sleep,
untold tales hiding their wings,
while outside in the summer dark
the wind howls like a woman in love.

You can hear the trees cry
as they bend toward ground,
pulpy fibers stretched to crack,
while the menses of the moon bleed pale,
phases lost like children
under the unloving sky.

These secrets hang upside down
like bats, fly unerringly in midnight fog,
swoop and clutch, shriek their darkness
with a razor smile,

but still, I will not tell.

Appassionato

It is like trying to chase the moon
as it crosses the western sky,
hoping to find the place
where finally it rests.

Or like searching for the thread
that holds words to song intact.
One or the other keeps floating
just above the page.

Or wandering without a clue
about which is north or south;
it might forever be circles
whose beginning is the end.

Whatever it is
it is like this:
putting one foot in front of the other
and starting all over again.

Interdental Processes[°]

It is amazing how phrases are born
squalling into the mouths
of those who did not plan them,
how they grow and change
and grow again, sometimes
disappear, lost and confused.

The drill whines on and on,
its high-pitched screaming
raising shivers and tooth-dust,
jaw numb as Lot's wife,
the price one pays
having looked back in vain.
Decay is an odor
that settles on time.

"Long in the tooth"
aged Bengal tigers
are called, lions,
old men, me.
The gums recede with age,
neglect, family history;
small ivory nuggets
now lengthened by nudity,
the pale pink pulp reduced
to little more than memory.

In a parched bid for language
we bring ourselves to this:
cut, prod, pull, all to stop
the words from losing themselves
in the dark vowels
of an empty mouth.

[°]Linguistically, the process by which consonants
are made, with the tongue against the teeth.

Just Killing Time

There is less of me these days.
Pieces are floating like jetsam
on the various seas.
Reports have been made
of a leg in Jersey,
a toe in Chicago,
a lock of hair swept by the Santa Ana's
clear across the west
up into Alaska.

Yet I lumber around
like a grizzly gone blind,
an astronaut in a moon suit,
feeling my weightlessness
a hindrance to movement,
lightning-quick responses
a thing of the past;
the air is so heavy
it takes forever to lift a hand
and wave goodbye.

Twelve Steps

One
Learn a new language,
say Russian or Japanese.
It will taste like vodka
or slippery gingered fish.

Two
Color your hair
brown or black,
fringe the sides,
let the curls hang straight.
Perhaps a streak of red.

Three
Walk only backwards,
never look ahead.

Four
Go out for dinner
and order eels.
Let your tongue slide
and stick over
every suckered piece.

Five
Call up three friends.
Tell them something
    anything
the others have said.
Turn out the lights.
Watch July in June.

Six
Take off all your clothes,
lie down in a pool,
float on your back.
When your skin peels
like an old potato
pluck out the eyes.
You're done.

Seven
Take a vow of silence.
Do not speak to anyone
for three whole days.
Try it again
this time for a week.
Notice how important
eyes have become.

Eight
Take a deep breath.
You're three-quarters there.

Nine
Begin old projects
never begun.
Give them as presents
to people unknown.
File the thank-you's
for later reference.

Ten
Sing a song
you don't know
with someone you do.
Laugh as you pick your teeth
with a string of waxen words.

Eleven
Go for a walk
in a perfect circle.
Find its radius
and cut across.

Twelve
If necessary,
go back to step one
and start all over
again.

I'm a Woman

a high woman
a low woman
a flat-footed woman
a woman who walks on walls
ceilings, over puddles
right through dreams woman
a brown-eyed woman
an olive woman
a denim woman
a frizzy woman
a frazzled woman
an impatient woman
a woman who can wait
a powerful woman
a cuddle woman
a talkative woman
an interrupting woman
a feeling woman
a caring woman
a selfish woman
who wants it all
but gives it back,
a dog-loving woman
cat-loving woman
child-loving woman
man-loving woman
a thinking woman
a writing woman.

I'm a moon-walking woman
a sun-diving woman
a cheerful woman
a weirdful woman
I'm a deep-seated woman
a three-seated woman
an unseated woman
I'm a sister, a mother
a daughter, a friend
but nobody's love.

I'm a blue sky woman
a stars-clouds-rain woman
a techno woman
a silly woman
a happy woman
a hit-the-deck-running woman
a fast driving, cooking, talking woman
a dancing woman
a music woman
a quiet woman
a clothes woman
an undressed woman
the kind of woman
who would seduce a priest
but never a child.
I'm a woman who knows
there is more to know
than can ever be known.
I'm that kind of woman.

Celestial Conversations

The moon, the stars, the sun,
they speak a language round
and filled with light.
It is orange and ochre,
ivory, bright as love.
It sounds like the sea,
soft and sibilant,
urgent and insistent.

It tells of the beauty in circles,
the globular o's of surprise,
the pleasure in elliptical patterns;
it points to the curve of belly, breast,
the cylindrical joints of elbow, knee,
the circumference of a toe,
the spherical nature of soul,
exalting speech as a gift.

Using the same words,
each has its own voice:
the sun's rich modulation,
its warm vowels, amber notes;
the moon's cool tone,
patterns like carved ivory,
intricate and fine; the high
sweet pitch of the stars.

Redemption

This is about
the spells cast on princesses,
the years they spend asleep.
How they awaken with a jolt
staring straight into the eyes
of some throbbing prince.

But this is not a fairy tale,
it is flesh and sweat.
There is sex and redemption,
violence and rapture.
There is moon and stars and wind,
there is a forest and a Big Bad Wolf.
But the woodcutter has a hard-on
and what he hacks is not for love.

There is thunder.
Storms polarize around me
like magnetic dust.
There is lightning and a vision.
There is the endless rain
that falls inside my heart.

Concentricities

You remember a long whistle,
a freight train at 3 a.m.
Wisconsin, Illinois, Indiana,
Kentucky, reverse and back again.

Sitting with coffee, you think
of circles—the world
is all circles—going and coming.
You wonder why it matters.

Outside, the trees are almost black
in their nakedness, the sky
white with clouds, the moon
a thin sliver of ice.

You suppose it is the distance,
the landscapes in between.
The way color changes
deep into night.

You stir the coffee
and watch the circles: concentric.
You lift your cup:
circles on the table.

You inhale, exhale: circles of smoke.
You look into his eyes: circles of doubt.
There's a geometric perfection
in all of this, if only

you had the formula down pat.
You doodle on the page,
remember degrees of arc
but that's as far as you get.

The train whistles again—
the same sound as before
and suddenly you want to buy a ticket,
go somewhere you've never been,

walk in straight lines
and never double back.
But you can't—it's always round-trip.
Another circle. And you've already been there.

Singing in the Key of L

It would be no use, they said; you're tone deaf,
they said, you sing in the key of L.
Lousy, limp, lame, L for sounds like 'ell.
Goodbye piano, goodbye guitar.

And though I had words for them all,
I could not string them along
in sweet and perfect pitch, and though I could
hear the soft and rounded rhythms, my voice
could not, would not, slide the alphabet
toward those acceptable seven keys.

But come moonlit nights, when the music in me
is too high to hear, along with dogs,
cats, crickets, and mosquitoes, I sing
loud and lusty, loud and free, inventing
new chords, and dance, dance, dance.

II. Duet

Songs are like people, animals, plants. They have genealogies, pedigrees, thoroughbreds, crossbreeds, mongrels, strays, and often a strange lovechild. —Carl Sandburg

Eventually

You will be dark, moon in your hair,
a crooked smile, nice teeth.
I have a passion for teeth.
See here? This perfect crescent on my thigh?
Made by you. It is faintly blue.
Your hands will be smooth,
but enough lines to cost you extra
in Madame Soutzaka's tent.
You will talk with those hands;
pictures hang like smoke.

You won't quite know
what to make of me,
only that you want
what I seem to be giving.
You will be drawn to my flecked eyes,
the sand in my words.
But there are complications.
Lives with their rituals and habits,
closets that can't be emptied,
fresh scars that have never scabbed.
You will want to see them turn black,
then pick them pink again.

Cybergames

Make me your computer.
Every time you turn it on
it's me; touch the keys
it's me, how do I feel?
Tell me how it feels.

Look at the screen.
Do you see me there
between the pixels
a crystal shimmer
in my liquid eye?

Move the mouse slowly,
it's your hand on my arm.
Click, you've touched
me, somewhere
out there, where it's safe.

Abracadabra

Sometimes the night comes on like a caul,
creeps in like a caterpillar
inching its long patient way
toward something else,
something hidden
behind the veil of stars,
behind the limits of our dreams.

What magic lurks in words—
darkly flowing lines that mean
nothing in themselves?
It is only illusion,
an agreement between fools.
An alchemist could do better
turning tin to gold.

One Night Stand

Everyone knows the world
consists of random acts,
who we are
as accidents of birth,
yet surrounded by order.
Think of the slow arc
of the sun, the even slower
arc of the moon, all lies
of course, perceptions we choose
to make real,
like this candle,
this bed,
this lonesome scrap of love.

A Million Names for Rain

Mostly it was the rain, I think
and the smoke and memories.
Yes, the rain and the moon.
It is never what you think.

So maybe it was something else—
maybe it started in the head,
moved slowly down the body,
the heart, the groin, the knees
which are always the worst; they buckle
and bend, like rubber bands
bounced back and forth, back and forth,

which is probably how we wound up
in bed after all that time;
nothing much worked anyway,
but that isn't the point—
the point is that it was summer
in Boston and raining,
dark and different from home.

But none of the names for rain
could ever explain
the color of that sky
or the smell from the bakery
across the street, us in that window
our feet on the fire escape,
watching the moon come and go
through breaks in the clouds
as if it thought
it really had a chance

Is the Middle Halfway In
Or Halfway Out?

A philosopher should be shown the door, but don't
under any circumstances, try it.   —John Ashberry

In the middle. Always
in the middle.
The thick of things
as it were.
Surrounded by youth
you hang
suspended
like a drop of golden oil
in a glass of blue water,
full at the bottom
and so overwhelmed.

There is a center
after all
and while you're in it
you manage to forget
who you are
or why.
And there's a center
to that center
where you're quiet
and alone, not being
anybody else at all.

The drums roll
and the guitarist slides
metal-wrapped fingers
along the strings.
Outside, lightning lashes
to memory, tightens
its hold, and refuses
to be split, like a tree

that bends, that says,
"I've had enough"
and refuses to be struck.

While you dance around
gathering disciples
who want to learn anything
about everything
because there's so much you know
and so much to give
and it's just so damn easy
to be the one to do it.

Changing the Direction of Dawn

What if suddenly the world
stopped spinning clockwise
paused
for just a moment
then started turning the other way?
Would everything go in reverse?

Would our present turn back
to become our past
before we had a chance
to remember?
Would we never be absolved,
no chance to atone?

Would the sun rise in the west,
the moon take over day?
Would we
wake up to pale light
sometimes golden, then silver?
It is so easy to love in the dark.

Making Love to a Cannibal

You can imagine the delicacy
such acts require.
Each nibble a loss:
an ear lobe, toe, small, tender ankle,
gone—all gone—each part
disappearing, like an ice cream
licked slowly away.

Yet caught as you are
by the passion of danger
you somehow don't notice
the parts that are missing
small price to pay
for being loved so well.

Then one morning you awake
stretched in the sun
and discover you're gone—
nothing left but a dent
next to the full-bellied man
with your smile on his face.

Mid-life Crisis #23

Don't you know there's a war on?
he says, and I look up
from my papers
square into his eyes
earnestly brown,
and I can tell
he's worried,
fine lines eroding his face,
the scar from the glass
I'd thrown once in anger
now redder, insistent.

I try to think, what war?
The war in the Gulf
over for more than a year?
The former Soviet Union?
Columbia? Haiti? L.A.?
There are little wars everywhere.
He is sitting down now
staring out the window.
Could he mean our war
against the carpenter ants?
I can't think what to say.

He seems content to just sit
and I notice the top of his head,
shining where the hair's gone,
his beard growing grey in the middle,
and his hands, lying lost
in his lap, red at the knuckles,
his once slim frame still small
but thickened at the belly,
his feet, knobby and splayed
like an old horse planted in pasture,
and suddenly I know which war.

I smile and take his hand,
raise it to my mouth,
gently kiss and put it back,
never having said a word,
for to speak would name it,

put a shape to his terror,
force him to do battle
windmills or no.

It is enough that while he sleeps
his breath whispers softly,
Dulcinea. Dulcinea.

The Other Woman

Does she ever see her
in a dream
holding her losses
like dead kittens
in her hands?

Does she hear her
sob in her sleep
the sound escaping
in a long shudder
through her abandoned mouth?

Can she smell her sorrow
like a stale cologne
clinging beneath
her untouched breasts,
the dry crevice between her thighs?

Does she know how pain grows
and grows until, like moss
it conceals everything, suffocating
the very stone beneath,
the last shreds of pride?

And does she, at last,
this other woman,
wonder what the wife,
bereft of even a phantom limb,
thinks about, all the rest of her life?

Etude (for Love)

First it is a pebble,
a smooth white round little thing.
Then it grows to a stone
and begins to roll,
every tumble an accretion,
a hardening of fact
until it is a rock
where it sits
a long, long time,
its shape altered
by wind, by rain, by tears.
But still it sits
and grows to a boulder,
angular and large,
covered in snow, in ice,
in leaves, in sand, in sun,
then a mountain,
a mountain so big
not even you could move it.

Tornado Warning

It isn't so much your little hands
turning my face to look,
the chicken pox scar left of center
on your forehead scattered
with corn silk, and eyes so blue
I drown each time I look.

It isn't that I'm amused,
grown older, wiser, can afford
to watch, smile at the innocence
of effusion, everything white
and pink and blue, of course,
except the sky.

It isn't why that night twice we went
into the laundry room
with my comforter for cover,
you laughing at the fun,
swept from bed and carried
to the safest room of the house.

But when you asked if the tomato
was going to rip our house,
it was then I knew no matter what
there would always be a room
I'd carry you to, even if it had no walls,
even if you didn't want to go.

Playing for Keeps

So it comes down to this:
a division of property.
You get Boardwalk;
I get Park Place.
Only it isn't quite that fair.
Yours has hotels, comfort.
Mine belongs to the Bank.
Pick a card, don't pass Go.

Or scramble the issues
then sort them out
letter by letter, point by point.
Why is twelve and triple
will get you thirty-six,
a tidy sum to balance your side.
Jezebel brings even more;
with a double, you're at fifty.

Whether you play high or low,
the Queen of Spades is thirteen points,
a heart is only one;
you either throw them away or pick them up,
pass left, pass right, across, and hold;
she might be worth the risk,
dangerous and forbidden,
but in this game, it's all or nothing.

The Cape Was Never White
Little Red Riding Hood

First of all, I was not skipping.
I never skip, but yes, I was eating
strawberries: red, ripe, delicious.
I had heard rumors
that girls who ate them
would never want for men.
I was after the woodcutter
not the wolf, but the wolf
was quicker, sly, and intense.
I hadn't meant to enjoy it—
but being swallowed whole
was a definite kick
no man could ever give.

Sonnet in Eight Beats

There is a gentleness to wind
to how it caresses the sun,
the trees, the pelicans and gulls—
see how they glide softly through sky—
watch the children's kites dip and sway
take off higher and higher still,
then sink in a pillow of cloud
only to fly again till reeled
slowly home, a moon on their tails
shimmering silver, then gold—then
the last embers of daylight gone
flutter down to the cooling sand.
    Like your touch, your blossoming mouth,
    the fragile memory of love.

Looking Back
Briar Rose

Any way you look at it
they're all animals
one way or another.
Mine even was one.
It wouldn't have been so bad—
even for the long snout,
the snaky tail;
no it was the hair,
so itchy, so alive,
so crawling with things
I dreaded most.

Sure my life was grand:
golden dresses and silk sheets,
a castle full of jewels,
and only the Beast and I.
Not that I was bored—
oh, no, I was well-entertained,
the nights too short to contain
the joy I discovered in dark.
And the garden! The roses!
Not a thorn to be found—
except for the hair
        that suffocating hair.

Storm Warnings

What is it they say
about red skies at dawn?
When the wind blows leeward
not even secrets stay still.
See how clouds gather
on the horizon, how flat
the sea seems faraway?
You could sail forever
and never catch up.

When the rains come,
they come hard, driving out the light,
sucking sound from a room
until all you hear is the roar,
the rush and beat of rain,
the long, low thunder rolling
like a wave, closer, closer
till it cracks the startled night.

You know there is trouble
when the lights go out
but you are drawn to danger,
like to watch the flash and fire,
the hunger of passion.
What does the wind want
when it slaps then kisses
and how much
are you willing to risk?

Sometimes what we say is true
and sometimes we just believe it.
You would think by now
we could tell the difference.

III. *Cantata*

Music, not being made up of objects nor referring to objects, is tangible and ineffable; it can only be, as it were, inhaled by the spirit: the rest is silence. —Jacques Barzun

Proverb: *If You Have Nothing Good To Say Then Keep Your Mouth Shut*

And she did. For days and days.
The silence turned into thunder
shaking the timbers of the house,
it raged, like Colorado rapids
after a torrential rain.
After several weeks without sound
its absence was deafening,
it broke glasses and windows,
cracked walls and foundations.
Months of steady jarring made
mounds of plaster build
quietly in corners. Soon
the house itself began to fall
until all that was left was rubble,
the color of blood.

Finding Myself in New Smyrna

Northern Florida has wide white sandy beaches
soft and powdery, not like the crushed shell down south.
There are cars, too, parked against the seawall like trees
(of which there are none) giving a hot metal shade
to the sandpipers and pigeons, the crabs and gulls
and one lone egret lost from its bovine roost
in pastures far to the west.

Perhaps the sound of sea, long rolling waves breaking
upon the shore enticed the bird to leave its back
and travel east, against the wind and strict advice
from family back home, warnings gone unheeded
for here he is, pecking softly at the wet sand
delighted with sea lice, crab, a minnow or two
instead of dry fleas, fat ticks
and inarticulate cows.

Sleeping with the Ants

Suddenly, from nowhere they come
crawling, flying, slapping soft
against my skin, translucent
wings across my cheek, breast,
tangle in my hair.

This is not the country,
I am not outside—
ants have no dominion
in my bed
so I swat, pinch

brush them to heaven
all the while itching
if only by suggestion,
one eye still reading,
the other crawling about

searching for movement,
a dark speck like a floater,
dust mote in the breeze.
Finally, unable to bear
the suspense, the jolt of touch

I attack with spray, mist
the room thick, close the door,
my lair abandoned,
driven out by one of hundreds
of thousands of species

who could drive me out
though smaller than a tooth,
a thumb nail, a lock of hair,
more powerful than light,
more insistent than tongues.

I return to an acrid sting
in my nose and throat,
to find them littered

on the carpet like so many
unknown warriors, without ceremony—

old memories of war, the odor
of gun powder, ozone depletion—
while I wander still warily around
checking sheets, pillows, stacks
of books that would condemn

my brute disregard
of the rights of all creatures,
the chemical bond with air
forever altered while I settle
back into bed, humble but triumphant.

Just the Rain Saying It All

It is raining.
It has been raining, days
of sad skies, swollen clouds
fog on the windows
as though children pressed
in their faces, breathing
designs against the glass,
a game for snowy days.
But it is nothing
so ethereal as white flakes,
original in their crystal form,
making you want to run
and catch them on your tongue,
the ice hot melt tasting of iron;
no, just rain, dull, grey, wet.

It is early afternoon
and the lights are on,
small lamps in the hall,
flourescents in the kitchen.
There is music, soft jazz,
what's known as progressive—
Richard Elliot, Enya, Yanni—
lots of sax and harp,
no lyrics to confuse the issues,
what's left to be said anyway?
Down to form, melody,
the simple purity of a clean note.
So it has come to this:
where words are no longer enough,
offer no message you want
to carry, fall in step to, proclaim.

Just the sound of the rain
and the sax and the harp
and your own assured breathing
as you wander the rooms
trapped by nature,
the perfect rightness of rain.

Pedestals

The problem with sculptors is this:
once they finish their work
they want to show it off
on cool, hard marble stands.
They spend long hours
in good light or bad
admiring it, turning it this way
and that, caressing the long curves,
polishing it to incredible gloss.
      And then it begins:
first a wayward grain of sand
imbeds itself, causes
a dullness in the sheen,
then a slight nick, a flaw in the finish.
Gone crazy with grief, some
will act quickly, a smooth
clean cut of the ax and it's over.
But others, blinded by art
sit heaped on the floor,
and slowly, nail file in hand,
scrape away at the base—
ten, twenty, fifty years.

Folding In

Somewhere between adolescence and middle age
you wake up, brush your teeth, dress,
put on your make-up, sip coffee
from your Go-cup, leave for work
and it happens
that sitting at a traffic light, a young man
cycles by, looks in your window,
mutters, "ugly bitch,"
and your breath sucks backward,
your heart skips two, maybe three beats
and you glance in the mirror,
realize he's right, it's true,
you are no longer whistle-worthy,
not even an appreciative glance
and your shoulders hunch,
your lips suddenly wrinkle
drawing tight little lines
across now-hollow cheeks,
aging quickly, suddenly
folding yourself into a sentence
longer than this one.

The Woman Who Talked
Till She Ran Out of Words

Vaccinated with a phonograph needle
her family said, she started early
and never stopped.
She talked through her thumb
her nails, her finger-picked lips,
her milk teeth, her straight teeth,
her teeth grown longer.
She talked loudly and fast
tumbling together an alphabet soup,
she talked while spooning,
sipping, chewing, smoking,
making hot little trails
around her words, paths
that led to sudden surprises.
She talked while working, thinking,
reading, even while loving,
her voice lower, softer, a little hoarse.
She talked while she laughed and cried,
grew up, grew old and died still talking
her mouth forever frozen as if to ask why.

Archaeology

Take, for example, this rock:
not round, yet not square,
a lump, really, of no shape.
It is not smooth, yet not harsh,
just sort of bumpy, pale
but not white, deckled
with age, a certain character.
It has no odor but a whiff of time,
perhaps a bit of earth.
Yet this rock, this lime, this shale
is entirely the world
speaking a language
long since gone to pebble.

Mutating Shapes

Like a dying star whose light
reaches us long after its gone,
her sight has turned inward,
swallowed by the black hole
her life has become, a whirling
vortex which pulls everything in
but lets nothing out.

"See that pole?" she points. "It bends
in the breeze. It dances
down toward the lake. Can you see?"
Curves come up to meet her now,
straight lines, like memory,
mutating into shapes
with names she never knew.

"Macular degeneration," the doctor said,
tender, but glib. She is not
after all, *his* mother, is not someone
he watches day after day
as she loses one by one
life's simple tasks.

I find her in her chair
by the window, a book open
in her lap. She has read
this same page all day,
the words colliding—
a galaxy of thought she can't hold still.

"Don't worry," she says, patting
my hand. "There's much to be learned
from words that won't stay formed."
And she's right. Watching her fingers
smooth the page, I listen. Never
has there been such eloquence
in the silent air.

Obsession Between the Sheets

What if the dictionary were really a novel?
Read beginning to end, what crisis
occurs in the middle?
Does a mad tom, overcome with a sense
of his own magnetic intensity
leap from his quiet lake in the north
and head down south for stone crabs?
Do all the women of the world
become Maenad's, attacking even Zeus?
And once the page is turned
and "magnitude" gives way
to various forms of "main,"
does anything get resolved?
Even the beginning is more complicated
than you'd think, with almost forty-five
definitions for "a," so you can imagine
what goes on after *that*.

Do all the words, mashed together
as they are between the sheets, start to mingle
reproducing more and more complications,
like rabbits or fleas hopping about?
Over two hundred thousand progeny
from only twenty-six choices.
And how does it end?
How symbolic is the length of "heart"
compared to that of "strike"?
Or the note on whether "unique"
isn't overused as a word?
What would the critics think?
Would they say that while it starts off
simply enough, it soon bogs down
in ambiguous baciliary characters,
deanimized against an ethereal landscape,
that the plot twists and turns
like a nervous snake,
the resolution resolving nothing,
yet demonstrating unparalleled verve

in its use of language?
What moral balance is obtained
from reading about xenophobes
and the zeitgeist of a generation
obsessed with clever acronyms?
Perhaps the only logical approach
is through deconstruction, after all,
taking each word for what it is,
only to find that there is no meaning,
each word just a word, a sound, a daisy chain
hung around our necks, our hair, blooming
prettily until it withers, then dies, winding up
at last, pressed between these pages once again.

Song of the Graiae°

I. Enyo

We have stopped playing games
and settled on a more reasoned
approach: every third day
I have the eye. It is blue
and wide as heaven.
The whole of the Aegean
fits in its depths.

Through it, I see the fertile sun,
how it dapples the meadow
the golden wheat shimmering
in and out of clouds,
my children romping
in the summer breeze.
We dance and sing in the light.

When I have the eye, I can see
myself in the polished stones,
I laugh and shout to my sisters,
those grey necked swans
who sit on their rocks all day
and sightlessly gaze at nothing.
I tell them to sing, but they won't.

They are brooding and jealous,
thinking only of their turn,
won't listen to my vision,
never tell me theirs.
They claim I'm too young,
would never understand,
but it is they who don't understand
the light, the shadows, the dreams
that keep me, even
when I cannot see.

°In Greek Mythology, three women
who shared one eye between them.

II. Dino

Every third day I sit on my bench
here by the sea, gazing at the patterns
made by the tide, the way it rolls,
then ripples, laps slowly to shore
lacing its edge with a fine cut work.
I am deliberately alone, knowing
the others will not venture this far
without sight, afraid of the crags,
the beautiful sharp edges
etched against a limitless sky.

The silly women will never see
how elegant is rock, how I long
to carve it, smooth and polish,
create the beauty I see on my days,
shape it like clay, breathe life
into its veins, its cool surface
molded from my hands.
They will never understand
the intricasies of stone, the subtle strength
running through ropy sinews,
how it breathes, warms to the touch,
how even when I can't see, I can
with my hands, how it remembers
my shape, holds me like a lover.

I have changed the landscape
again and again, each time more
grand, and get only complaints
from my two stumbling sisters
who lose their way, can never adjust,
never appreciate how hard I try
with my one brown eye to brighten
this forsaken place, this island
no one ever truly sees.
Perhaps if I build shining white cities,
someone will come, take me away,
leaving those weeping-haired hags
to bump loudly in the night, alone.

III. Pemphredo

Those stupid ninnies.
Look at them, uselessly gazing
into this grey, cold mist.
They think I don't hear them
mumbling their dreams, gibberish
nonsense that makes me laugh.

We are alone here, utterly and forever
alone, but they walk around talking
to the sea, the stones, the grey clouds
that block even the dullest bit of sky.
The youngest sings lullabies
cradling a rock in her arms;
the other crouches all day
scratching at air and rock.
All that's here is rock,
nothing else, except the sea,
the colorless stretching sea,
and this misted shroud
that gives no warmth.

They think I don't know
what they're doing, they think
I'm the one who's mad.
Wait till it's my turn again;
I'll make them look
deep into my obsidian eye
swallow them up
and feed them truth,
nothing but truth.
Forever.

The Philosopher Mechanic

If truth is really truth, he said,
then it is unchanging, eternal;
we are born knowing everything.

Impossible, I argued, leaning
carefully on the worn counter,
my feet drawing circles in the sawdust,

the smell of oil and carburetors
equally loud in nose and ears,
amazed at this man
in starched, stained shirt,
greasy pants, soft insistent voice
between me and the other customers,

two worlds at odds with a normal day.
Think about it, he said, handing a woman
the keys to her Toyota,

the truth was always the truth,
even before perception made us aware;
therefore, we always knew it

even if we didn't think we did.
So how come, I said smugly,
there isn't a cure for AIDS?

But there is, he countered, there is.
The doctors know it, but haven't
combined it yet, haven't thought

in terms of truth, the truth in the life
of a microorganism, the fact
that nothing ever dies because

it is all part of truth, and truth
is eternal, unchanging, immortal,
so they're merely looking in the wrong place.

I stared at him while he ran
a credit card through a machine,
gave out receipts, answered the phone.
I've always believed, I said,
that the more I learn,
the more I learn what I don't know.

He smiled a sad little smile.
But that's just it, he said,
you already know everything.

I shook my head and gave up,
wandered off to check on my car,
wishing he were right

because if he were, I could
have saved $131.37
and fixed the damn antenna myself.

Creating Our Past

Listen, sister, here is the key.
See how it is rusted
to a dull orange stain,
a moon unused to wishes.

And here is the book,
small in its ivory cover
that once was white,
once had roses growing outside.

Now there is only one
pressed in the back,
the color of blood
washed from sheets.

As the pages are turned,
you will smell the basement
after the last big flood,
the cage where our hamsters

in their consuming passion
consumed each other,
the box of field mice
we tried to save.

There, too, are the socks
we hunted for father,
little brother's bit of finger
shaved by glass.

Mother's voice will drift into light,
released from the nights that held it,
sweet and low, like the distant train
that carried our dreams away.

She will be dressed in the Chinese silk
embroidered with peacocks,
her hair abundant and dark,
her laugh like warm milk.

And sister, look at our brothers,
tall and straight and still,
nothing they couldn't do
stuck to them like skin.

And the lilacs and tulips,
the white pompoms we called snowballs
and the hollyhocks and lilies of the valley
we couldn't wait to pick.

They are all here.
Here, too, is the future,
the one where I find you
where I never knew to look.

Barbra Nightingale has a Master's of Arts in Literature from Florida Atlantic University, and a doctorate in Higher Education from Florida International University. She is a professor at Broward Community College, where she teaches English, American Literature, and Poetry. In 1997, she was awarded the James L. Knight Endowed Teaching Chair. She is the author of three chapbooks: *Lovers Never Die* (1981, Lieb/Schott Publications), *Prelude to a Woman* (1986, Earthwise Press), and *Lunar Equations* (1993, East Coast Editions). Her poems have appeared in numerous journals, including *Kansas Quarterly, The Chattahoochee Review, The Birmingham Review, Blue Light/Red Light, The MacGuffin, The Poet, Many Mountains Moving, Calyx, The Florida Review, Kalliope,* and *Cumberlands Poetry Review.* She lives in Hollywood, Florida.